TRADITIONS AND CELEBRATIONS

100 TH DAY OF SCHOOL

by Sharon Katz Cooper

PEBBLE
a capstone imprint

Pebble Explore is published by Pebble, an imprint of Capstone.
1710 Roe Crest Drive
North Mankato, Minnesota 56003
www.capstonepub.com

Library of Congress Cataloging-in-Publication Data is available on the Library of Congress website.
ISBN: 978-1-9771-3183-6 (library binding)
ISBN: 978-1-9771-3285-7 (paperback)
ISBN: 978-1-9771-5376-0 (ebook PDF)

Summary: On the 100th Day of School, some students make crafts or play counting games to mark the event. Others learn about life 100 years ago. Or they imagine how it would feel to be 100 years old! No matter what, the day is a fun way to mark 100 days of learning.

Image Credits
iStockphoto/SDI Productions, 27; Shutterstock: 1000Photography, 28, 13Smile, cover, 1, Carolyn Dietrich, 11, Dmitry Zimin, 8, GagliardiPhotography, 13, GUNDAM_Ai, 23, Haver, 12, Janthana, 18, Lapina, 17, LiliGraphie, 25, Monkey Business Images, 6, 9, 15, Nigmatulina Aleksandra, 10, OnlyZoia, 22, Photographee.eu, 7, Robbie Proctor, 19, Robert Kneschke, 29, udra11, 20, William Graziano, 4, Yuriy Golub, 21

Artistic elements: Shutterstock/Rafal Kulik

Editorial Credits
Editors: Jill Kalz and Julie Gassman; Designer: Juliette Peters; Media Researcher: Kelly Garvin; Production Specialist: Spencer Rosio

All internet sites appearing in back matter were available and accurate when this book was sent to press.

TABLE OF CONTENTS

Words in **bold** are in the glossary.

WHAT IS THE 100TH DAY OF SCHOOL?

Do you have family **traditions**? Does your town have traditions? What about your school? There are many traditions around the world.

In the United States, many schools **celebrate** the 100th Day of School. Everyone starts counting on the first day of school. The 100th Day is around the end of January. Sometimes it is early February.

Students and teachers celebrate with parties. They play games and do special schoolwork. It is a lot of fun!

The 100th Day of School is a **milestone**. Many teachers celebrate what students have learned so far. Students make a list of things they have learned. They choose their favorite things!

Some students make a big **mural**. They draw 100 things they love about their school.

They also talk about what they will learn the rest of the year. What are the students looking forward to? What would they like to learn next?

CELEBRATING IN MATH

Math is an important subject in school. The 100th Day is a time to learn about the number 100. It is a big number!

Young children practice counting. They count jelly beans or other candies—and then eat them!

Some teachers make a chart on
the wall. Students count each day of
school until they get to 100. Teachers
ask students to sing or dance. They
count to 100 at the same time.

Some students count 100 stickers
to put on a crown. They wear their
crowns all day. These are special
100-Days crowns.

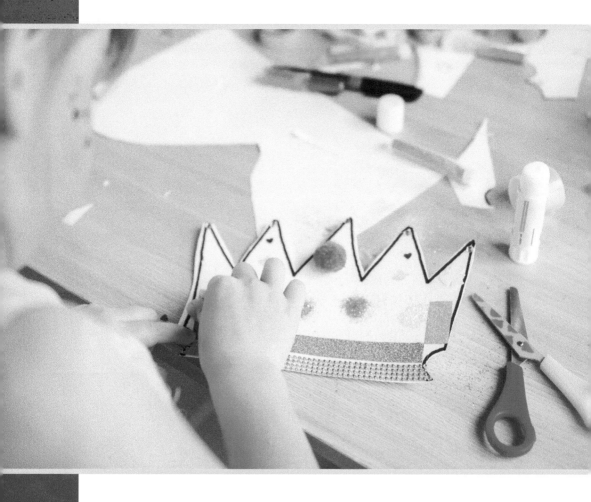

How about measuring and weighing? Do 100 pennies weigh the same as 100 balls of cotton? Students collect the items and find out!

Students explore other math questions. How many years until you turn 100? How about your parents? Or your grandparents? Students do the math for each person.

Estimation is a great math skill. Teachers fill jars with different numbers of candies or pennies. Students estimate how many objects are in each jar. Who can guess which jar has 100 things in it?

Older students write **equations** that add up to 100. For example, 1+99, 23+77, and 25x4 all equal 100. They talk about ways to count to 100. They count by ones or fives or tens. Can you do that?

CELEBRATING IN WRITING

In writing class, students write 100 words they know. They might write poems with 100 letters. They might read a story about the number 100.

Some teachers ask their classes to read 100 books by the 100th Day. Everyone works together! The class begins counting at the start of the school year. Students keep track on a big group list. Students add books they have read to the list. When the class makes it to 100, everyone gets a prize!

Some teachers give students writing ideas. What will you do when you are 100 years old? What will the world look like in 100 years? If you had $100, what would you do with it?

Students write short stories about these things. What would you write about?

100 DAYS IN SCIENCE

There are many 100th-Day ideas in science class. Students build towers with 100 objects. They use popsicle sticks or cups. A teacher might **challenge** students to build a house with 100 blocks.

Students make **collections** of objects. They might collect 100 shells or leaves or pennies. They fill small bags or jars with these objects. Students collect their objects until the 100th Day. Then they show the class what they have. What 100 things would you collect?

100 DAYS IN ART

In art class, students make long paper chains. They add 100 paper rings. Students make special 100-Days T-shirts. They put 100 things on their shirts. These things could be safety pins or buttons. They might use googly eyes or sparkles. Students choose!

Everyone wears their shirts to school on the 100th Day. They march in parades around the school.

Students **decorate** their classrooms. Some students make snowflakes out of paper. They hang them up around the room. They count 100 snowflakes!

Some students string 100 beads to make a necklace. They can be colorful. They share these necklaces with their friends. Students also put together 100-piece puzzles. Are those hard or easy?

100 DAYS IN HISTORY

History is fun to explore on the 100th Day. What was the world like 100 years ago? What things were the same? What was different? What did people wear? What did they eat? What did kids do for fun? What was school like?

Students dress up as a person who lived 100 years ago. What would you wear?

100 DAYS IN GYM

How about gym class? Students celebrate 100 days here too! Teachers might challenge students to do 100 jumping jacks. Or 100 push-ups. They run 100-meter dashes. Some students toss a beanbag 100 times. Some walk 100 steps on the playground. They measure how far that is.

Teachers might ask students to count their steps every day. On the 100th Day, they see how far they walked in 100 days.

Teachers and students look forward to the 100th Day of School all year! There are so many amazing ways to celebrate. How does your school celebrate 100 days? Can you think of some new traditions? There are at least 100 ways to celebrate!

GLOSSARY

celebrate (SEL-uh-brayt)—to do something fun on a special day

challenge (CHAL-uhnj)—to invite or dare to take part in a contest

collection (kuh-LEK-shuhn)—a group of objects that have something in common

decorate (DEK-uh-rayt)—to add things to make something prettier or stand out more

equation (i-KWAY-zhuhn)—a math sentence using numbers

estimation (es-tuh-MAY-shuhn)—making guesses by using the information you have

milestone (MILE-stone)—an event that marks a special change

mural (MYOOR-uhl)—a large piece of art on a wall

tradition (tra-DIH-shuhn)—a custom, idea, or belief passed down through time

READ MORE

Carson, Emma Berne. *100th Day of School*. North Mankato, MN: Cantata Learning, 2018.

Mortlock, Michele. *What Were the Roaring Twenties?* New York: Penguin Workshop, 2018.

Rabe, Tilsh. *The 100 Hats of the Cat in the Hat: A Celebration of the 100th Day of School*. New York: Random House Books for Young Readers, 2019.

INTERNET SITES

100th Day of School
enchantedlearning.com/themes/hundred.shtml

Kids Math
ducksters.com/kidsmath/

100th Day Videos
simplykinder.com/100th-day-videos/

INDEX